Cat

# Cat

LAUGHING ELEPHANT BOOKS          MMII

# CATS are a blessing, and make our lives richer through their companionship. We, in turn, bless them and the homes in which they reside.

First, there is the special wonder of kittens –
tumbling, innocent, vulnerable, exquisite;

and the sweetness of mother cats with their babies.

We always enjoy their grace
and beauty of form,

which they maintain both when in movement
and in stillness,

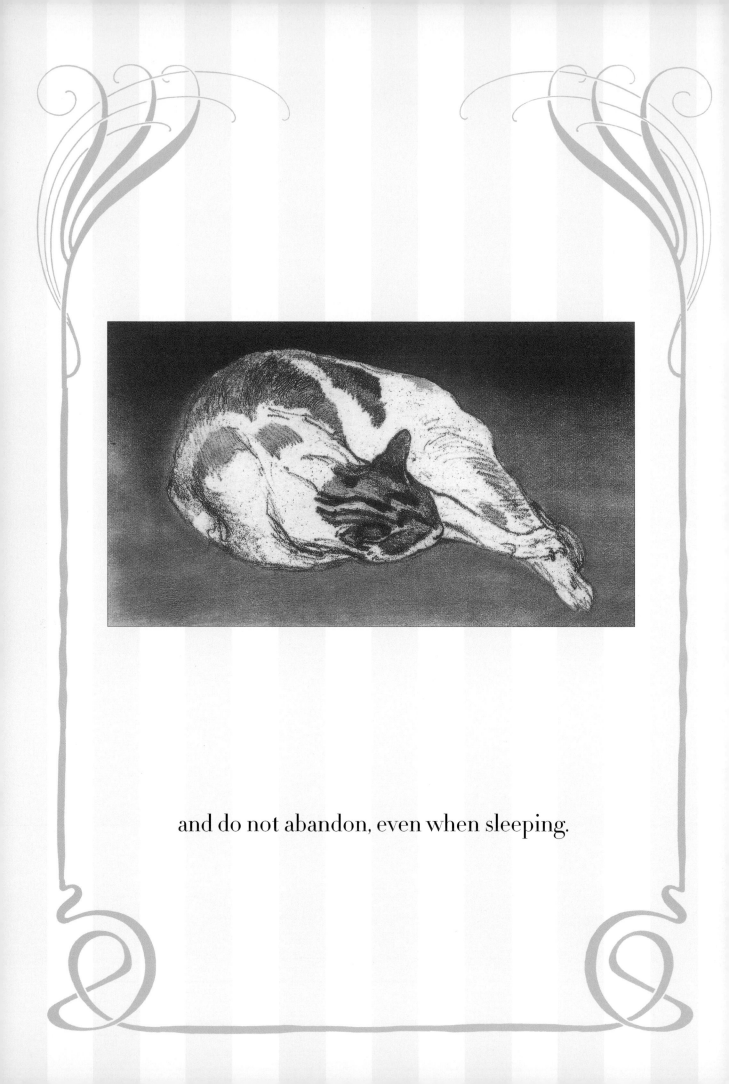

and do not abandon, even when sleeping.

Cats have a profound dignity

and great patience.

They live fully, enjoying without reservation
each moment of each day.

They are intensely curious,

which can lead to trouble, even disaster.

We envy them for their profound contentment,

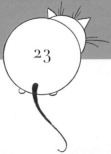

and their alert and poised stillness.

Our cats are fine companions. They ask little,

but are silently and reliably beside us,

gracing our lives through their beauty.

# Picture Credits

# Picture Credits

# Colophon

Designed at Blue Lantern Studio
by Sacheverell Darling & Mike Harrison

Typeset in Didot & Bickham Script